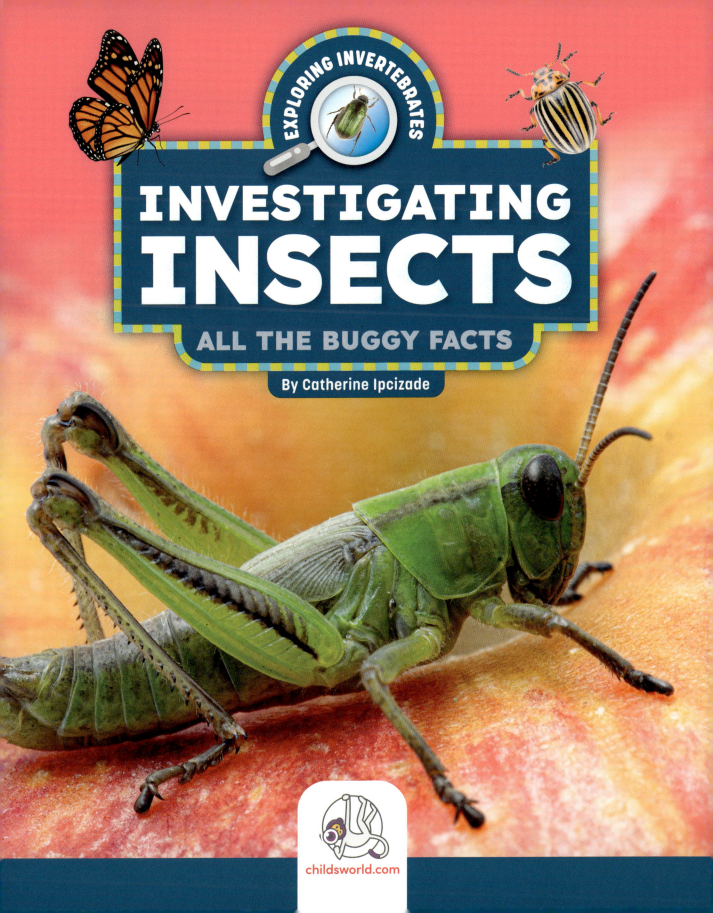

Published by The Child's World®
800-599-READ • childsworld.com

Copyright © 2025 by The Child's World®
All rights reserved. No part of this book may be reproduced or utilized in any form or by any means without written permission from the publisher.

Photography Credits
Cover: ©©alonanola/Shutterstock; ©Jiang Zhongyan/Shutterstock; ©Georgy Dzyura/Shutterstock; ©Shin Okamato/Shutterstock; ©Reynold Mainse/Design PIcs/Getty Images; page 3: ©LeManna/Shutterstock; pages 4–5, 9: ©Konstanttin/Shutterstock; pages 4–5, 24: Bernatskaia Oksana/Shutterstock; page 5: ©irin-k/Shutterstock; page 5: ©prapat1120/Shutterstock; pages 5, 12: ©1st-ArtZone/Shutterstock; page 5, 23: ©Evgeny Parushin/Shutterstock; pages 6–7: ©Romacho/Shutterstock; page 7: ©Eric Isselee/Shutterstock; page 8: ©Subbotina Anna/Shutterstock; pages 8–9, 17: ©Henrik Larsson/Shutterstock; page 9: ©optimarc/Shutterstock; pages 10–11: ©Oasishifi/Shutterstock; page 13: ©janith priyasanka/Shutterstock; page 14: ©Inkholy/Shutterstock; page 14: ©BlueRingMedia/Shutterstock; pages 14–15: ©NeagoneFo/Shutterstock; page 15: ©zcw/Shutterstock; page 16: ©Jolanda Aalbers/Shutterstock; page 18: ©Chase D'animulls/Shutterstock: page 19: ©DanielPrudek/iStock/Getty Images; page 19: ©Dimijana/iStock/Getty Images; page 20: ©Mark Brandon/Shutterstock; page 21: ©irin-k/Shutterstock; page 22: ©Lori Bye

ISBN Information
9781503894471 (Reinforced Library Binding)
9781503894747 (Portable Document Format)
9781503895560 (Online Multi-user eBook)
9781503896383 (Electronic Publication)

LCCN
2024941371

Printed in the United States of America

ABOUT THE AUTHOR

Catherine Ipcizade is a college professor and the author of more than 30 books for children. She loves photography, cooking, and spending time with her family in sunny California and the mountains of Utah. Her favorite word is "serendipity" because life is full of unexpected, fortunate surprises.

CONTENTS

CHAPTER 1
MEET THE INSECTS! 4

CHAPTER 2
A CLOSER LOOK . . . 8

CHAPTER 3
LIFE CYCLE . . . 12

CHAPTER 4
INSECTS IN THE WORLD . . . 17

CHAPTER 5
KEEPING INSECTS SAFE . . . 20

Wonder More . . . 21
Finding Its Wings . . . 22
Glossary . . . 23
Find Out More . . . 24
Index . . . 24

CHAPTER 1

MEET THE INSECTS!

It's a sunny spring day. A butterfly glides past a bee on a flower. Ants march in a straight line on the ground. These are insects. Insects are **invertebrates**. That means they don't have backbones. Insects have a hard outer shell called an **exoskeleton**. It's like their very own built-in suit of armor!

Insects come in all shapes and sizes. They have six legs and often have two sets of wings. Most insects are about the size of a paper clip, but some beetles and flies are smaller than a grain of salt. The giant Goliath beetle can grow up to 10 inches (25.4 centimeters) long. That's bigger than many adult shoes!

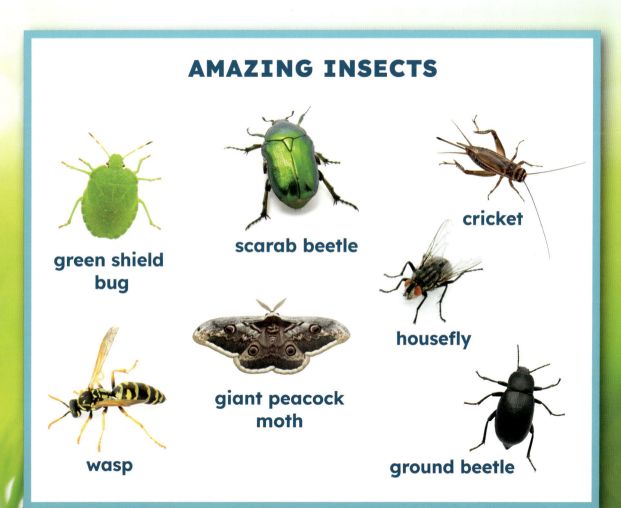

AMAZING INSECTS

green shield bug

scarab beetle

cricket

housefly

wasp

giant peacock moth

ground beetle

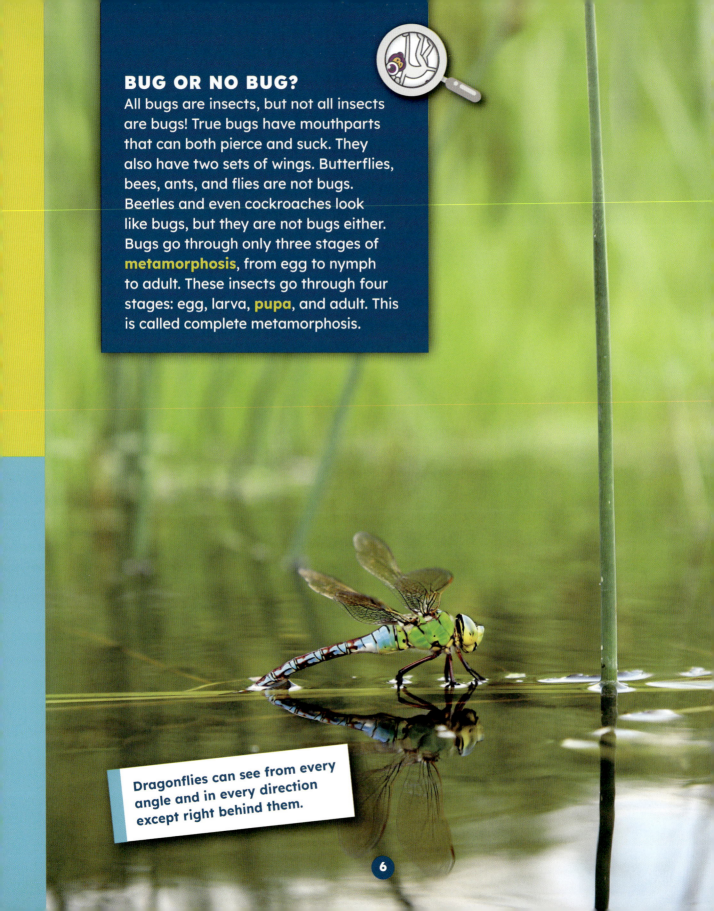

BUG OR NO BUG?

All bugs are insects, but not all insects are bugs! True bugs have mouthparts that can both pierce and suck. They also have two sets of wings. Butterflies, bees, ants, and flies are not bugs. Beetles and even cockroaches look like bugs, but they are not bugs either. Bugs go through only three stages of **metamorphosis**, from egg to nymph to adult. These insects go through four stages: egg, larva, **pupa**, and adult. This is called complete metamorphosis.

Dragonflies can see from every angle and in every direction except right behind them.

Insects are picky eaters. Flies have taste buds on their feet! Butterflies sip sweet **nectar** from flowers. Grasshoppers like to munch on leaves. Adult mayflies don't even eat at all! Insects are unique and live all around us.

Around 97 percent of all the animals on Earth are invertebrates. That's a lot of crawling and buzzing! Insects are the largest group of invertebrates, and there are more beetles than any other insect. They love to dig and burrow underground. Butterflies use their wings to flutter through sunny meadows and forests. Ants travel in lines back to their underground nests. Bees live underground or in busy, buzzing beehives.

Many insects live on land, but some even make their homes in fresh water.

CHAPTER 2

A CLOSER LOOK

Insects might not have backbones, but that does not stop them from moving in all sorts of ways! They can walk, crawl, fly, and even jump! Many insects also have amazing vision. While humans can only see in front of them and a little on each side, insects have **compound eyes**. They can see all around—nearly 360 degrees!

    A cicada nymph climbs into a tree. It rests on a branch. Soon, it will shed its skin and emerge with wings. This is called **molting**. Many insects shed their exoskeleton in order to grow. It can be a dangerous time while they wait for their new shell to harden because they are easy targets for **predators**. It's a good thing their new shells harden quickly.

INSECT SIZE COMPARISON

Hercules beetle
Body length: 2 to 3.35 inches (50 to 85 millimeters)
Body width: 1.14 to 1.65 inches (29 to 42 mm)
Body height: 0.47 to 1.42 inches (1.2 to 3.6 cm)

Seven-spot ladybug
Length: .24 to .31 inches (6 to 8 mm)
Height: .1 to .14 inches (2.5 to 3.6 mm)
Width: .16 to .22 inches (4 to 5.6 mm)

Ants can carry up to 50 times their own body weight. When they need to lift more, they work together as a group.

WAGGLE THIS WAY

Insects aren't just busy. They are also smart! Honeybees use a special "waggle dance" to tell other bees where to find food. The scout bee waggles, and the other worker bees know where to go. The waggle dance tells them not only where to go, but also in which direction they should move. That's a powerful dance by a little bee.

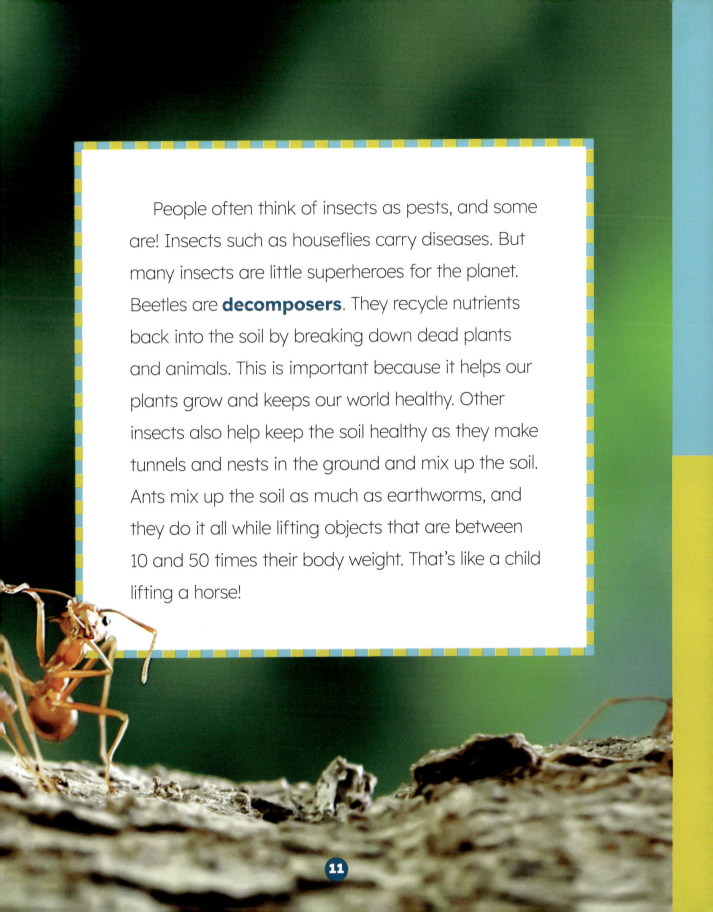

People often think of insects as pests, and some are! Insects such as houseflies carry diseases. But many insects are little superheroes for the planet. Beetles are **decomposers**. They recycle nutrients back into the soil by breaking down dead plants and animals. This is important because it helps our plants grow and keeps our world healthy. Other insects also help keep the soil healthy as they make tunnels and nests in the ground and mix up the soil. Ants mix up the soil as much as earthworms, and they do it all while lifting objects that are between 10 and 50 times their body weight. That's like a child lifting a horse!

CHAPTER 3

LIFE CYCLE

In the insect world, some creatures fly alone, while others live and work together. Butterflies, grasshoppers, beetles, and dragonflies don't need a leader or a community to survive. They take care of themselves and find food on their own.

But some insects, such as flies, thrive on teamwork. Bees and ants live in colonies, sometimes with thousands of members. Colonies are like tiny cities where everyone works together to make sure things run smoothly. These colonies have a queen bee or a queen ant. The queen is the leader. She lays eggs so the colony keeps growing. In ant colonies, some ants are soldiers who protect the colony, while others are workers who make sure everyone has enough to eat.

Queen bees have longer bodies and shorter wings than the hive's other bees.

Insects can lay one egg or thousands of eggs at a time. A queen termite can lay 30,000 eggs in one day! Because insects are small and vulnerable to predators, laying so many eggs helps to ensure that their **species** survives.

Insects live and grow in unique ways. Their life cycles are also unique. Mayflies only live for one day. But some queen termites can live for 50 years!

Many insects go through metamorphosis. This means their bodies change into new shapes as they grow. Moths start as an egg. Then, they hatch into a caterpillar. The caterpillar makes a **cocoon** and changes into a pupa. The pupa opens, and out comes a colorful moth.

FROM EGG TO MOTH

Egg   Larva   Pupa   Adult

TAKING FLIGHT

Instead of a cocoon, an adult butterfly emerges from a chrysalis (KRIS-uh-lis). But it does not fly right away. First, the butterfly must stretch. It hangs from the chrysalis to open its wings. The butterfly stretches its abdomen to pump fluid into its wings. This helps the wings to fully open. After an hour or two, the butterfly is ready to fly. Most butterflies live for two to four weeks.

Although it starts out green, a chrysalis turns brown or orange when it is almost time for a butterfly to emerge.

A ladybug's bright color is a warning to predators. If a bird or other insect eats a ladybug, they might get sick!

CHAPTER 4

INSECTS IN THE WORLD

When insects fly, crawl, and buzz around, they are often helping the **ecosystem**. You've just learned that some insects, including bees and butterflies, are pollinators. Other insects, such as beetles, are decomposers. Most insects are food for birds, bats, fish, and other animals that need them to survive. And some insects are predators themselves. Ladybugs eat 50 or more aphids each day. As a result, plants are healthier.

Bees have one of the most important jobs in the ecosystem. When a bee sips nectar from a flower, the **pollen** from that flower sticks to the bee's fuzzy legs and body. When the bee visits the next flower, some of the pollen from the first flower sticks to the new flower. Without buzzing bees, plants could not keep growing. And without growing plants, people would not have many of the fruits and vegetables they eat today.

Humans can help bees do their important work by planting flowers that bloom in summer and early fall.

When bees visit flowers, they collect pollen with their bodies. They take it back to their hive for food, but some gets left behind on other plants, which helps them grow.

CHAPTER 5
KEEPING INSECTS SAFE

Some insects are pests. But most insects are important for life on Earth. From pollinators to decomposers, insects play important roles in the planet's ecosystem. Even insects that are eaten by other animals provide a food source and keep the food chain strong and healthy.

People can help insects do their jobs by protecting them and keeping their homes safe. This means not using harmful chemicals nearby. It means letting decomposers and recyclers do their jobs. Every creature has a place on the planet, and that includes insects!

WONDER MORE

Wondering about New Information

What information about insects surprised you? Write down two facts that you learned from this book. What was the most unexpected fact you learned?

Wondering How It Matters

Insects have different roles that keep our environment healthy. Why is this important? What would happen if all insects performed the same job?

Wondering Why

Why do you think living in colonies is helpful to ants? What are some of the different roles that exist in an ant colony?

Ways to Keep Wondering

After reading this book, what questions do you have about insects? Which insects would you like to learn more about? What can you do to learn more about them?

FINDING ITS WINGS

Butterflies are all around us! But they didn't start out as butterflies. In this activity, you'll go through the four stages of metamorphosis to show how a caterpillar becomes a butterfly.

Steps to Take

1) Fold a piece of paper into four squares.

2) Label the top left square EGG.

3) Label the top right square LARVA.

4) Label the bottom left square PUPA.

5) Label the bottom right square ADULT.

Supplies
- pencil
- paper

Using your pencil, draw a picture in each box that shows what the insect looks like at each stage of the metamorphosis process.

GLOSSARY

cocoon (kuh-KOON) A cocoon is a covering or case made by some animals that protects them as they grow.

compound eyes (KOM-pownd EYES) Compound eyes are made of many individual units.

decomposer (dee-kom-POH-zur) A decomposer is a creature that breaks down dead organisms in soil or water into smaller particles.

ecosystem (EE-koh-sis-tum) An ecosystem is a group of creatures and environments that work together.

exoskeleton (EX-oh-skell-ih-tun) An exoskeleton is an artificial external supporting structure.

invertebrates (in-VER-tuh-bruts) Invertebrates are animals that do not have a backbone.

metamorphosis (met-uh-MOR-fuh-sis) Metamorphosis is a change of physical form or structure.

molting (MOHL-ting) Molting occurs when an insect sheds its outer layer.

nectar (NEK-tur) Nectar is the sugary substance in flowers that bees collect to make honey.

pollen (PAHL-lin) Pollen is a fine dust in a seed plant.

predators (PRED-uh-turs) Predators are creatures that get food by killing and consuming other organisms.

pupa (PYOO-puh) A pupa is an immature insect, the stage just before reaching adulthood.

species (SPEE-sheez) A species is a group of living things that are able to reproduce.

FIND OUT MORE

In the Library

Davidson, Lauren. *The Backyard Bug Book for Kids: Storybook, Insect Facts, and Activities!* Emeryville, CA: Rockridge Press, 2019.

Johnston, Sharman. *Insects for Kids.* Emeryville, CA: Rockridge Press, 2022.

Markle, Sandra. *Locusts.* Minneapolis, MN: Lerner Publications, 2021.

On the Web

Visit our website for links about insects:
childsworld.com/links

Note to Parents, Caregivers, Teachers, and Librarians: We routinely verify our web links to make sure they are safe and active sites. So encourage your readers to check them out!

INDEX

ant, 4, 6–7, 10–12, 21

beetle, 4–7, 9, 11–12, 17
bug, 5–6
butterfly, 4, 6–7, 12, 15, 17

eggs, 6, 12–14
eyes, 8

food, 10, 12, 17, 19–20

ladybug, 9, 16–17
legs, 4, 18

moth, 5, 14

wings, 4, 6–8, 13, 15